modern

FABRIC ART BOWLS

Express Yourself with Quilt Blocks, Appliqué, Embroidery & More

KIRSTEN FISHER

C&T PUBLISHING

Text copyright © 2021 by Kirsten Fisher

Photography and artwork copyright © 2021 by C&T Publishing, Inc.

Publisher: Amy Barrett-Daffin

Creative Director: Gailen Runge

Acquisitions Editor: Roxane Cerda

Managing Editor: Liz Aneloski

Editor: Kathryn Patterson

Technical Editor: Debbie Rodgers

Cover/Book Designer: April Mostek

Production Coordinator: Tim Manibusan

Production Editor: Jennifer Warren

Illustrator: Linda Johnson

Photo Assistant: Lauren Herberg

Photography by Estefany Gonzalez of C&T Publishing, Inc., unless otherwise noted

Published by C&T Publishing, Inc., P.O. Box 1456, Lafayette, CA 94549

Library of Congress Cataloging-in-Publication Data

Names: Fisher, Kirsten, 1950- author.

Title: Modern fabric art bowls : express yourself with quilt blocks, appliqué, embroidery & more / Kirsten Fisher.

Description: Lafayette, CA : C&T Publishing, [2021]

Identifiers: LCCN 2020038976 | ISBN 9781644030295 (trade paperback) | ISBN 9781644030301 (ebook)

Subjects: LCSH: Fabric bowls. | Quilting--Patterns. | Appliqué--Patterns. | Embroidery--Patterns.

Classification: LCC TT835 .F5724 2021 | DDC 746.46/041--dc23

LC record available at https://lccn.loc.gov/2020038976

Printed in the USA

10 9 8 7 6 5 4 3 2 1

DEDICATION

This book and most of the quilting patterns we use today would not be possible if not for all the math teachers who taught us about angles and measurements, especially my own high school math teacher at Klostergade Skole in Vejle, Denmark: Mr. Sven Aage Poulsen. He made math fun and simple. When I set out to transform a 12″ quilt block into a 3-D shape and had to work with odd angles and measurements, it was all so much easier because I had learned from him that a math problem is a fun challenge. I came to appreciate the intricate math required to create the many quilt blocks we use today, developed by quilters—primarily women—who were never given credit for their skill. This book is dedicated to them.

ACKNOWLEDGMENTS

This book was not created in a vacuum.

When I first decided to share the technique I developed in a book, many members of the Brooklyn Quilters Guild encouraged me, especially Martha Musgrove and Chris Janove.

Over the years I have formed strong bonds with some quilters who, like me, have also studied with Nancy Crow. They became my support group. Madeleine Appell and Martha McDonald went above and beyond. Madeleine simply wouldn't accept me not writing the book and made sure I knew it. I can't thank Martha McDonald enough for the hours of encouragement, support, and her calm steadiness.

I also want to thank the women in the Mapula Project in Pretoria, South Africa. I am grateful to the artists who did the beautiful embroidery used in this book, Jennifer Du Preez who encouraged the idea, and Janetje van der Merwe, whose help and many hours of hard work made it possible to show how the technique in this book can be used in an unexpected way.

Thank you to Anne Feldballe from Huset Anne Feldballe, Copenhagen, for some of the beautiful fabrics used in my bowls.

My greatest support in all of this has been my husband, Kenneth. From the day we met many years ago in Copenhagen, he has always believed in me and encouraged me to follow my path as an artist.

Thank you to C&T's terrific editors, Kathryn Patterson, and the other professionals who gave me this opportunity.

contents

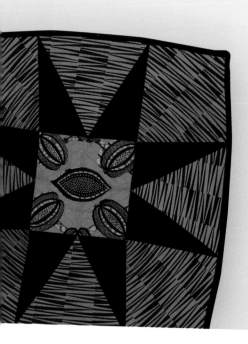

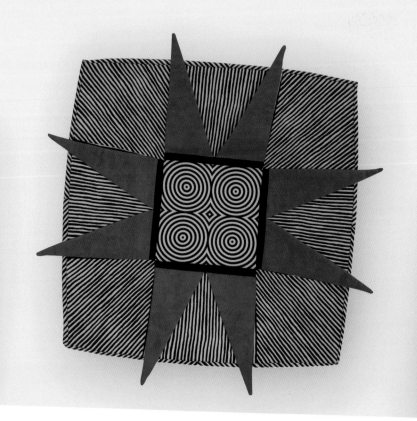

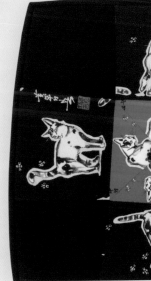

chapter 1

INTRODUCTION

A simple need started my love for fabric bowl making. In 2003, when my mother was 89 years old, she complained that she couldn't remember where she left her house keys. I set out to make a small bowl where she could always leave the keys. Because my mother loved the Ohio Star quilt block, I decided to make that block into the three-dimensional shape of a bowl. The bowl was made pretty much like a one-block quilt with patchwork inside, a solid backing, and interfacing as the batting. It was before I discovered fusible interfacing, so it was very loose, but it served its purpose.

Since then I have perfected the technique and made many bowls in many different sizes based on some of my favorite quilt blocks and also on some of my own abstract designs.

My very first fabric bowl

HOW FABRIC BOWLS ARE MADE

This book can be used both by the quilter who wants to use a traditional quilt block in a quick project and by the quilter who wants to experiment with shape and design in a three-dimensional form. No sewing experience is necessary, but it helps.

Each bowl can be made in four different sizes. The sizes given in the instructions are the pattern sizes. The finished dimensions of the bowls will vary depending on fabric choices and corner construction, but these are the approximate sizes:

Size	Diameter	Height	Circumference
18″	16½″	6¼″	57″
15″	13½″	4¼″	48″
12″	10½″	3¼″	38″
9″	7½″	2¾″	29″

The largest size makes for a perfect cat bed!

Bowls can be made without the use of a sewing machine. If you sew a bowl by hand, you may choose not to secure the center base and corner seams of the outside layer, so make sure the fabric is securely fused to the interfacing and finish the bowl with a fold-over binding.

These fabric bowls are easy to make; just follow the directions one step at a time. Each bowl consists of fabric and two layers of heavyweight interfacing—an outside layer and an inside layer, fused together. Because each layer is made separately, the inside and outside designs will be different. You can personalize the two layers in many different ways. And you can decide whether or not to quilt them. Quilting is not necessary, but it can be an added design element. Once you have mastered the basic techniques, you can use your imagination to personalize your bowls.

The basic steps to making each layer are similar. First, draw the pattern without seam allowances on the double-sided heavyweight fusible interfacing and cut it out. Then fuse the cut-out pieces of interfacing to the wrong side of your fabric. Next, trim the fabric, allowing for a seam allowance around the edge of the interfacing. Sew the pieces together and you have created one layer for the bowl. Repeat these steps to make the second layer. Fuse the two layers together, add a binding, and you have made your bowl.

Chapters 2, 3, 4, 5, 10, and 11 are general instructions used for all the bowls. Chapters 6, 7, 8, and 9 are instructions for the individual insides of specific bowls.

Before starting to make a bowl, be sure to read Chapter 3: Basic Techniques for All Bowls (page 12).

Start by making the outside layer. For specific directions, go to Chapter 4: The Outside Layer (page 18). After the outside layer is done, go to the chapter for the project you want to make.

DESIGN INSPIRATION

Bowl made with one piece of fabric

Bowl made with striped fabric

Bowl made with scraps

The bowls are very fabric driven. One piece of beautiful fabric can make a fantastic inside of a bowl. Bright fabrics with a large floral pattern make fast bowls.

Another simple design can be created using a striped fabric and making the inside design out of four triangles.

The bowls are perfect for using up scraps.

Quilt blocks based on a nine-patch also work great for the inside design.

When designing the inside of the bowl, keep in mind that it will be seen from all four sides. It is not like a quilt with an up and a down as well as a left and a right.

THE CRUCIAL CENTER SQUARE

It is easier to design the center square first and then work out the rest of the design around the center square. The center square can be one piece of interesting fabric or it can be pieced, made of triangles, or appliquéd.

MINIMIZING BULK

Because the seams are hidden between the interfacing pieces, try not to make the pieces in the design smaller than 1″ × 1″.

If the design is made up of many small pieces, sew the fabric pieces together first and fuse that larger piece to the interfacing.

An inside layer made up of many small pieces

NOTE: Working with Curves
Heavyweight interfacing does not stretch. If the inside design has pieced curves, first sew the fabric pieces together and then fuse that piece to the interfacing.

chapter 2
SUPPLIES

Modern Fabric Art Bowls

HEAVYWEIGHT DOUBLE-SIDED FUSIBLE INTERFACING

I have used both fast2fuse HEAVY Interfacing (by C&T Publishing) and 72F Peltex II Ultra Firm Two-Sided Fusible (by Pellon), but I prefer fast2fuse HEAVY Interfacing. It is the firmer of the two interfacings and makes a much sturdier bowl. It is also easier to use when fusing the fabric to the interfacing because the fabric does not need to be covered by a damp pressing cloth. fast2fuse is available by the yard in 20″-wide bolts and as a packaged piece that is 15″ × 18″ or 20″ × 20″.

TIP If your interfacing does not lie flat, you can place it under a cutting mat with some weights on it for about 24 hours.

COTTON FABRIC

You should wash all your fabric before using it, especially if you plan to use dark cottons, so that the color does not run when you fuse it to the interfacing using steam or a damp cloth. Always iron your fabric before you fuse it to the interfacing so there are no wrinkles or fold lines.

NONSTICK IRONING SURFACE

Make sure that your nonstick surface, such as a Goddess Sheet or parchment paper, is larger than the piece of interfacing you are working with.

TIP If you use parchment paper, you can clamp it to the ironing board using binder clips. That way it will not slide when you fuse the fabric to the interfacing.

ADDITIONAL BASICS

Iron

Ironing board

Cutting mat, 24″ × 24″ or larger

Quilter's ruler, 6½″ × 24″ or larger

Rotary cutter with 60 mm or 45 mm blade

Template plastic *or* Quilt Bowl Corner acrylic template (See Resources, page 79.)

Pencil

Pins

Seam ripper

Sewing machine *or* quilter's betweens needles size 9 if hand sewing

Machine sewing needles sizes 80/12 and 90/14

40- and 30-weight threads to match the fabric

Pressing cloth (This can be any piece of light-colored cotton.)

ScotchBlue Original Painter's Tape (by 3M; *not* the delicate surface kind)

Fabric Grippers (by Nifty Notions; available at most quilt shops or online)

Optional: Square ruler 1″ larger than the bowl you are making (This is helpful but not required.)

NOTE

Some chapters have additional materials lists, depending on the bowl design.

chapter 3
BASIC TECHNIQUES FOR ALL BOWLS

FUSING FABRIC TO INTERFACING

All the bowls in this book are made using double-sided heavyweight fusible interfacing.

1. Cover the ironing board with a nonstick surface like parchment paper. This is important because the fabric is being fused to double-sided fusible interfacing.

2. Place the interfacing with the guidelines down on the nonstick surface. The guidelines are lines drawn on the interfacing as you create the pattern.

3. Cover the interfacing with the fabric, right side up. Make sure that the fabric is centered and there is at least 1″ of extra fabric all the way around the interfacing.

4. Fabric will give a little when it is fused to heavyweight interfacing, so begin by gently pressing the fabric and the interfacing together. This will not fuse them together; it will only align them and remove the wrinkles. With the iron on the wool heat setting, start slowly pressing from the center of the piece out toward the edges. Make sure there are no wrinkles in your fabric.

5. After the fabric has been pressed to the interfacing, fuse them together following the manufacturer's instructions. Don't put pressure on the iron, as it will leave indentation marks. Continue pressing until the fabric is securely fused to the interfacing. Let the piece cool before you move it.

TRIMMING FABRIC

These directions are for the inside layer and outside layer with directional fabric. For an outside layer made with one piece of nondirectional fabric, go to Chapter 4: The Outside Layer (page 18).

After the fabric is fused to the interfacing pieces, use a quilter's ruler and rotary cutter to trim the extra fabric down to ¼″ from all the edges of the interfacing, unless otherwise noted. With a precise ¼″ seam allowance it is easier to sew the seams.

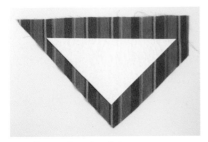

Interfacing fused to fabric

Trimmed fabric

SEWING PIECES TOGETHER

This is the general technique for sewing the seams. All seams are sewn with a ¼″ seam allowance.

1. Line up the top and bottom pieces so the interfacings of both pieces are perfectly aligned.

2. Pin the pieces together along the edge of the interfacing. This is to avoid any gaps between the pieces when they are sewn together.

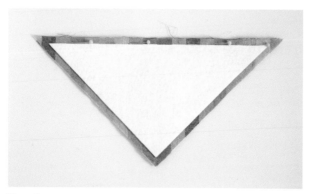

Top piece

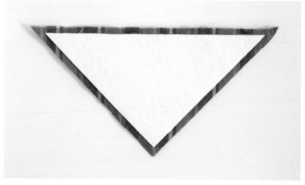

Bottom piece

3. Begin sewing from the edge of the fabric and sew right against the edge of the interfacing. That way there will be no gap between the pieces.

The seam will be between the 2 pieces of interfacing.

Sew right along edge of interfacing.

Two pieces sewn together

4. When 2 seams meet, line up the pieces, matching the seams, and pin before pinning the rest of the seam together.

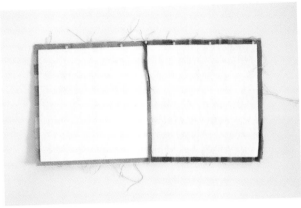

Connection seams pinned

Connection seam sewn

Sew the Seams for a Layer Made with Pattern 1

The shape of any bowl layer made with Pattern 1 is created by 4 corner seams. When making a layer with 4 triangles, sew the triangles together to make a flat square first. After sewing the seams to make the flat square, sew the 4 corner seams.

For instructions on using a corner template to trim the wedges from the corners of the interfacing, see Mark and Cut Out the Corner Wedges (page 21).

1. Fold the layer in half, fabric sides together. Use pins to hold the 2 sides together.

> **NOTE**
> Any quilting should be done *before* corner seams are sewn.

2. Pin and sew 2 opposite corner seams first, stitching right against the edge of the interfacing.

Layer folded in half and first 2 corner seams sewn

3. Repeat for the 2 remaining corners.

Last 2 seams pinned

NOTE

The layer will not lie flat after the first 2 seams are sewn. Therefore, it is very important to pin well along the edges of the interfacing before you sew the seams.

4. With a quilter's ruler and rotary cutter, trim the seams to ¼" from the edge of the interfacing.

Trimmed corner seam

Sew the Seams for a Layer Made with Pattern 2

The shape of any bowl layer made with Pattern 2 is created by the diamond shape of the 4 corner pieces.

Secure the Center Square

1. Sew the 9 prepared pieces into 3 rows of 3 pieces each.

2. Pin the side piece of one of the edge rows to the center square.

3. Sew the seam. Begin and end at the corner of the interfacing. Start at point A and sew just to point B. Do not extend the seam into the seam allowance.

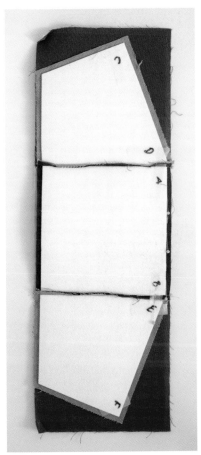

Sewn seam of center square

4. Repeat Steps 2 and 3 to attach the side piece of the remaining row to the center square.

Sew the Seams of the Diamond Shapes

1. Pin the diamond shapes together at the corner seams, pinning as close as you can along the interfacing edge at the side of the layer to hold the 2 side edges together. Place a pin along the interfacing edge at the beginning and end of the seam.

Pinned corner seam

2. Stitch the seam, backstitching at the beginning and end of each seam.

SEAMING ORDER

1. Sew the 2 seams on the same side of the layer.

Seam 1: Sew from the edge of the fabric at point C to the corner of the center square, point D.

Seam 2: Sew from the corner of the center square, point E, out to the edge of the fabric at point F.

Note that the layer will not lie flat, so pin as closely to the interfacing as you can.

Sewn first and second seams

2. Repeat seam 1 and seam 2 for the other side of the layer, completing the bowl shape.

chapter 4
THE OUTSIDE LAYER

The outside layer consists of 1 layer of heavyweight double-sided fusible interfacing and the fabric for the outside of the bowl. First, the pattern for the outside layer is drawn on the interfacing and is cut out. The fabric and interfacing are then fused together. The last step is sewing the 4 corner seams.

materials

A fat quarter is an 18″ × 20″–22″ cut of fabric.

HEAVYWEIGHT DOUBLE-SIDED FUSIBLE INTERFACING

18″ bowl: ⅝ yard or 1 package of fast2fuse HEAVY 20″ × 20″

15″ bowl: ⅝ yard or 1 package of fast2fuse HEAVY 20″ × 20″

12″ bowl: ⅜ yard or 1 package of fast2fuse HEAVY 15″ × 18″

9″ bowl: ⅜ yard or 1 package of fast2fuse HEAVY 15″ × 18″

FABRIC WITHOUT DIRECTIONAL PRINT

18″ bowl: ⅝ yard

15″ bowl: ⅝ yard or 1 fat quarter

12″ bowl: ½ yard or 1 fat quarter

9″ bowl: ⅜ yard or 1 fat quarter

FABRIC WITH DIRECTIONAL PRINT

Extra fabric may be needed to match a print or stripe.

18″ bowl: ⅝ yard

15″ bowl: ½ yard

12″ bowl: ½ yard

9″ bowl: ⅜ yard

EXTRAS

1 square 8″ × 8″ of template plastic or Quilt Bowl Corner acrylic template (See Resources, page 79.)

40-weight thread to match your fabric

Machine sewing needles sizes 80/12 or 90/14

cutting

HEAVYWEIGHT DOUBLE-SIDED FUSIBLE INTERFACING

18″ bowl: Cut 1 square 19″ × 19″.

15″ bowl: Cut 1 square 16″ × 16″.

12″ bowl: Cut 1 square 13″ × 13″.

9″ bowl: Cut 1 square 10″ × 10″.

FABRIC WITHOUT DIRECTIONAL PRINT

18″ bowl: Cut 1 square 22″ × 22″.

15″ bowl: Cut 1 square 19″ × 19″.

12″ bowl: Cut 1 square 16″ × 16″.

9″ bowl: Cut 1 square 13″ × 13″.

FABRIC WITH DIRECTIONAL PRINT

18″ bowl: Cut 4 identical rectangles 8½″ × 20″ and 1 square 7″ × 7″.

15″ bowl: Cut 4 identical rectangles 7½″ × 17″ and 1 square 6″ × 6″.

12″ bowl: Cut 4 identical rectangles 6½″ × 14″ and 1 square 5″ × 5″.

9″ bowl: Cut 4 identical rectangles 5½″ × 11″ and 1 square 4″ × 4″.

PREPARE THE CORNER TEMPLATE

If you are working with template plastic, trace the quilt bowl corner pattern (page 74) for the bowl size you are making onto the plastic; then cut it out on the traced lines to create a corner template. Skip this step if you are using the Quilt Bowl Corner acrylic template.

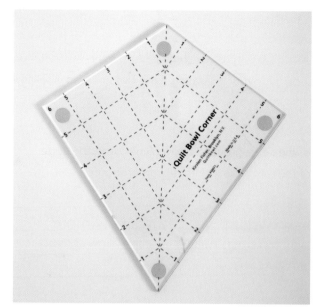

Quilt Bowl Corner acrylic template

PREPARE THE INTERFACING

Mark the following guidelines:

18″ bowl: Draw a line 6½″ from each of the 4 sides.

The center square should measure 6″ × 6″.

15″ bowl: Draw a line 5½″ from each of the 4 sides.

The center square should measure 5″ × 5″.

12″ bowl: Draw a line 4½″ from each of the 4 sides.

The center square should measure 4″ × 4″.

9″ bowl: Draw a line 3½″ from each of the 4 sides

The center square should measure 3″ × 3″.

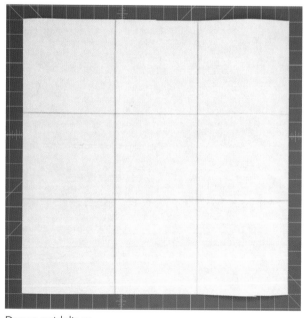

Drawn guidelines

Mark and Cut Out the Corner Wedges

To create the shape of the bowl, a wedge is cut out of each of the 4 corners.

1. Align the centerline of the corner template with the vertical line of the top right corner square so the tip of the template is at the corner of the center square. Draw a line along the edge of the template inside the corner square.

2. Move the corner template to the other side of the corner square and draw a line along the edge of the template inside the corner square. This makes 2 lines in the corner square.

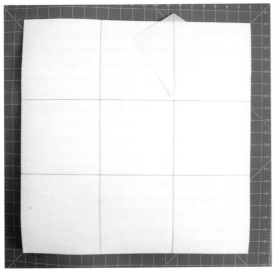

Preparing to mark first corner line

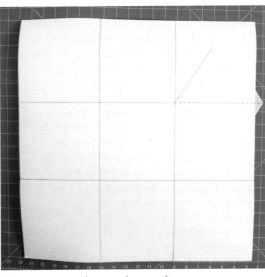

Preparing to mark second corner line

3. Use a ruler to extend the pencil lines out to the edge of the interfacing. Repeat for all 4 corners.

4. With a rotary cutter and a quilter's ruler, cut out the 4 corner wedges.

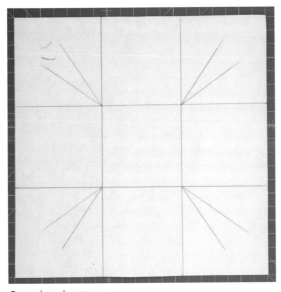

Completed pattern

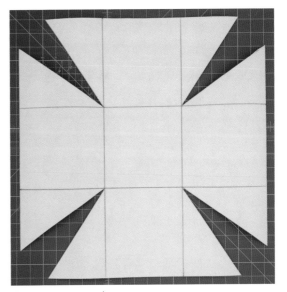

Cut out corner wedges.

TIP *Save the cutout corner wedges. Use them later to check how your fabric fuses to the interfacing and also to check the tension on your sewing machine.*

Draw the Cross Lines

Draw 2 diagonal lines in the center square.

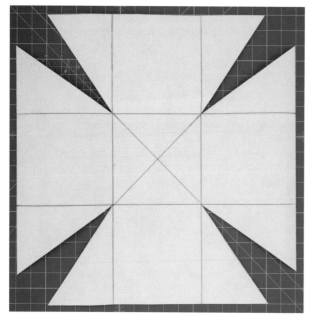

Center square cross lines

ADAPTING THE PATTERN FOR DIRECTIONAL FABRIC

The outside layer does not have to be made with a single piece of fabric. If working with directional fabric, you might want the fabric to go in the same direction on all 4 sides of the bowl. If you are using directional fabric for the outside of the bowl, you will have to change the pattern a bit. With a quilter's ruler and a rotary cutter, cut out the center square.

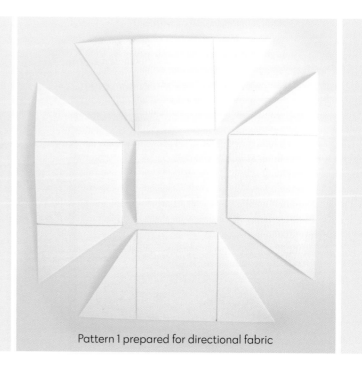

Pattern 1 prepared for directional fabric

FUSE THE FABRIC

> **NOTE**
> If you want to add a label to the bottom of the bowl, sew the label onto the center of the right side of the fabric before it is fused to the interfacing.

For step-by-step directions on how to fuse fabric to the interfacing, see Fusing Fabric to Interfacing (page 13).

TRIM FOR BINDING

The fabric is trimmed differently depending on the type of binding used to finish the bowl. It can be finished with either a fold-over binding or an add-on binding.

Fold-Over Binding

After the fabric has been fused to the interfacing, use a rotary cutter and quilter's ruler to trim the fabric to 1″ from the edge of the interfacing on all 4 sides. *Do not trim the fabric inside the corner wedges.*

Fabric trimmed for fold-over binding

Add-On Binding

With a rotary cutter and quilter's ruler, trim the fabric to the edge of the interfacing on all 4 sides. *Do not trim the fabric inside the corner wedges.*

Fabric trimmed for add-on binding

SCORE THE CENTER SQUARE LINES

With the tip of a seam ripper, score the lines around the center square. Also score the cross lines.

TIP *To ensure straight lines, run the seam ripper along a ruler. This makes it easier to fold the interfacing when you sew the corner seams.*

> **NOTE**
> For directional fabric, it is not necessary to score the seams around the center square.

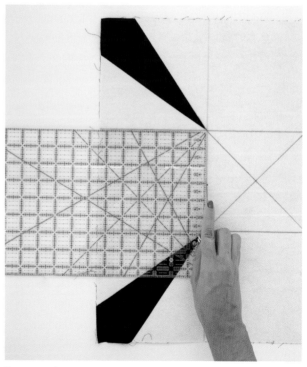

Score center square.

SECURE THE FABRIC TO THE INTERFACING

1. Using 40-weight thread and a 80/12 sewing machine needle, sew a straight stitch in regular length on the line around the center square that was just scored. If hand sewing the bowl, a strong, thin needle with a sharp point, like a quilter's between size 9, works best. *Do not stitch the cross lines in the center square.*

TIP *Pull up the bobbin thread at the beginning and end of the stitching so it doesn't get tangled in the seam.*

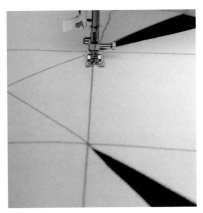

Secure the center square.

2. Sew a running stitch ¼″ from the edge of the interfacing at each corner-wedge cutout. Start at the left side of the corner and sew down to the line of the center square. Sew across the corner of the center square and back up the right side of the corner. Repeat for all 4 corners.

NOTE

These stitches are the only visible stitches on the bowl. This gives the bowl a finished look and ensures the fabric does not come loose from the interfacing as you continue sewing the bowl. Again, pull up the bobbin thread so it doesn't get tangled in the seam.

Secure corners for fold-over binding

Secure corners for add-on binding

TIP *With a fabric marker, draw lines extending the edges of the interfacing out to the edges of the fabric on both sides of each corner wedge. Those lines are helpful when sewing the corner seams.*

3. If you want to quilt the outer layer of the bowl, follow the instructions in Quilting (page 69).

SEW THE CORNER SEAMS

1. Fold the layer in half along the diagonal line so the fabric is inside and the interfacing is on the outside.

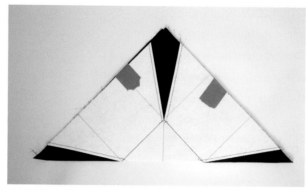

Folded in half, right sides together

2. Line up the corner tips of the interfacing's top and bottom layers. For the add-on binding version, hold the 2 sides together using quilter's clips or blue painter's tape. For the fold-over binding version, pin the 2 sides together.

TIP *Because you can't see the bottom layer of interfacing, use your thumb and index finger to feel when the tips of the interfacing's top and bottom layers are lined up.*

3. Pin right along the edge of the interfacing, with the tips of the pins pointing away from the center square. Check to make sure the pins run right along both the top and bottom layers of interfacing.

Corner seam pinned for fold-over binding version

Corner seam pinned for add-on binding version

Bottom layer of pinned seam

4. Sew 2 opposite corners first. For the fold-over binding version, sew from the edge of the fabric toward the corner of the center square. For the add-on binding version, sew from the edge of the interfacing toward the corner of the center square. Remove the pins as you sew.

TIP *To prevent gaps in the corners, it is very important to sew right next to the edges of both the top and bottom layers of interfacing.*

5. Refold the interfacing and repeat Steps 2–4 to sew the 2 remaining corners. *Do not press the seams with an iron.*

> **NOTE**
> After the first 2 corners have been sewn, the bowl will not lie flat. Just make sure the seam area is lying flat when you sew it.

Sew right along edge of interfacing.

TRIM THE CORNERS

With a rotary cutter and quilter's ruler, trim the fabric in each of the 4 corners to ¼˝ from the edge of the interfacing. You cannot trim all the way to the corner.

Trimmed corner for add-on binding version

Turn the outside layer right side out, and the outer bowl is finished!

Finished outside layer

chapter 5
THE INSIDE LAYER

This chapter gives general instructions for making all inside layers. The pattern for the inside layer is drawn onto heavyweight double-sided fusible interfacing. The pattern is then cut out, following the directions for the bowl you are making. The individual pieces of interfacing are fused to the fabric, the fabric is trimmed, and then the pieces are sewn together to create the inside layer.

For specific instructions for the inside layer, refer to the pattern and sewing directions for the bowl you are making.

materials

HEAVYWEIGHT DOUBLE-SIDED FUSIBLE INTERFACING

18″ bowl: ⅝ yard or 1 package of fast2fuse HEAVY 20″ × 20″

15″ bowl: ⅝ yard or 1 package of fast2fuse HEAVY 15″ × 18″

12″ bowl: ⅜ yard or 1 package of fast2fuse HEAVY 15″ × 18″

9″ bowl: ⅜ yard or 1 package of fast2fuse HEAVY 15″ × 18″

FABRIC

See the requirements for the bowl you are making (Chapters 6, 7, 8, and 9).

cutting

HEAVYWEIGHT DOUBLE-SIDED FUSIBLE INTERFACING

18″ bowl: Cut 1 square 18″ × 18″.

15″ bowl: Cut 1 square 15″ × 15″.

12″ bowl: Cut 1 square 12″ × 12″.

9″ bowl: Cut 1 square 9″ × 9″.

FABRIC

See the requirements for the bowl you are making (Chapters 6, 7, 8, and 9).

PREPARE THE INTERFACING

Mark Guidelines

18″ bowl: Draw a line 6″ from each of the 4 sides.

The 9 squares should each measure 6″ × 6″.

15″ bowl: Draw a line 5″ from each of the 4 sides.

The 9 squares should each measure 5″ × 5″.

12″ bowl: Draw a line 4″ from each of the 4 sides.

The 9 squares should each measure 4″ × 4″.

9″ bowl: Draw a line 3″ from each of the 4 sides.

The 9 squares should each measure 3″ × 3″.

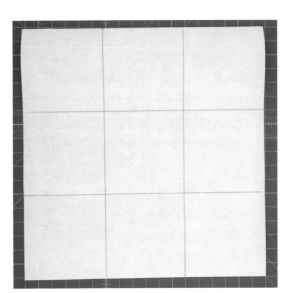

Drawn guidelines

Pattern 1: Mark and Cut Out the Corner Wedges for Corner Seams

1. Align the centerline of the corner template with the vertical line of the top right corner square so the tip of the template is at the corner of the center square. Draw a line along the edge of the template inside the corner square.

2. Move the corner template to the other side of the corner square and draw a line along the edge of the template inside the corner square. This makes 2 lines in the corner square.

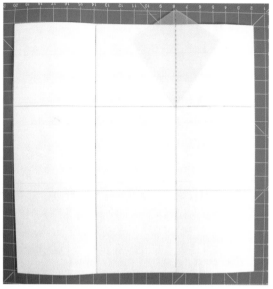

Preparing to mark first corner line

Preparing to mark second corner line

3. Use a ruler to extend the pencil lines out to the edge of the interfacing. Repeat for all 4 corners.

4. With a rotary cutter and quilter's ruler, cut out the 4 corner wedges.

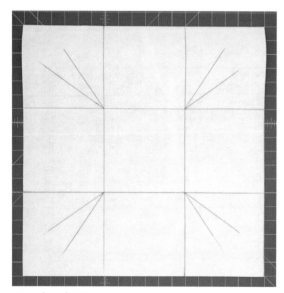

Completed Pattern 1

Cut out corner wedges.

TIP *Save the cutout corner wedges. Use them later to check how your fabric fuses to the interfacing and also to check the tension on your sewing machine.*

Pattern 2: Cut Out the Squares for Diamond Corners

With a rotary cutter and quilter's ruler, cut the 9 squares.

18″ bowl: Cut 9 squares 6″ × 6″.

15″ bowl: Cut 9 squares 5″ × 5″.

12″ bowl: Cut 9 squares 4″ × 4″.

9″ bowl: Cut 9 squares 3″ × 3″.

9 squares cut out

Trim the Diamond Corners

1. Select the corner template for the bowl size you are making. Trace the template on 4 of the interfacing squares.

Corner template on interfacing

Outline drawn

2. With a rotary cutter and quilter's ruler, cut out the diamond shapes.

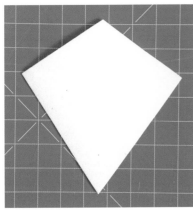

Cut out diamond shapes.

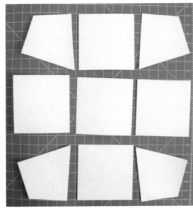

All interfacing pieces cut out

chapter 6
ONE-CLOTH WONDER BOWL 1

This pattern works great with a beautiful fabric piece with one large motif.

It also works well with an inside design that is appliquéd or embroidered.

materials

A fat quarter is an 18″ × 20″–22″ cut of fabric.

HEAVYWEIGHT DOUBLE-SIDED FUSIBLE INTERFACING

18″ bowl: ⅝ yard or 1 package of fast2fuse HEAVY 20″ × 20″

15″ bowl: ⅝ yard or 1 package of fast2fuse HEAVY 15″ × 18″

12″ bowl: ⅜ yard or 1 package of fast2fuse HEAVY 15″ × 18″

9″ bowl: ⅜ yard or 1 package of fast2fuse HEAVY 15″ × 18″

FABRIC

Extra fabric may be needed to match a print or stripe.

18″ bowl: ⅝ yard

15″ bowl: ½ yard or 1 fat quarter

12″ bowl: ⅜ yard or 1 fat quarter

9″ bowl: ⅓ yard or 1 fat quarter

cutting

HEAVYWEIGHT DOUBLE-SIDED FUSIBLE INTERFACING

18″ bowl: Cut 1 square 18″ × 18″.

15″ bowl: Cut 1 square 15″ × 15″.

12″ bowl: Cut 1 square 12″ × 12″.

9″ bowl: Cut 1 square 9″ × 9″.

FABRIC

18″ bowl: Cut 1 square 19″ × 19″.

15″ bowl: Cut 1 square 16″ × 16″.

12″ bowl: Cut 1 square 13″ × 13″.

9″ bowl: Cut 1 square 10″ × 10″.

PREPARE THE PATTERN

The pattern and directions for a bowl with just 1 piece of fabric as the inside layer are very similar to the directions for outside layers but with some minor changes.

See Pattern 1: Mark and Cut Out the Corner Wedges for Corner Seams (page 30).

TIP *For an inside layer with a centered motif, like a giant flower, make sure the fabric is cut so the motif is at the center of the fabric square.*

> **NOTE**
> For an appliqué or embroidery inside layer, see Appliqué and Embroidery (page 61).

FUSE THE FABRIC

After the pattern has been cut out, the fabric is fused to the interfacing. Follow the instructions in Fusing Fabric to Interfacing (page 13).

> **NOTE**
> After the fabric has been fused to the interfacing, do not score around the center square.

TRIM THE FABRIC

With a rotary cutter and quilter's ruler, trim the fabric to ¼" from the edge of the 4 interfacing sides. *Do not trim inside the corner wedges.*

> **NOTE**
>
> If you want to quilt the inside of the bowl, see Quilting (page 69).

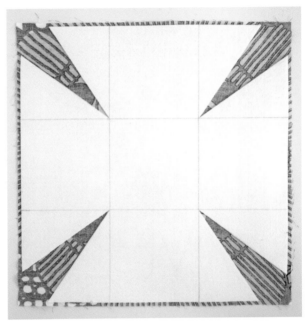

Trimmed fabric

SEW THE CORNER SEAMS

See Sew the Seams for a Layer Made with Pattern 1 (page 15).

Inside layer of One-Cloth Wonder

chapter 7
FUN WITH TRIANGLES
BOWL 2

Striped fabric works great for an inside layer with a design based on triangles.

The stripes can run either horizontally or vertically.

Pattern 1 is drawn onto the interfacing

and is then altered

to create four triangles.

Inside layer made of 4 fabric triangles

Bowl with vertical lines

Bowl with horizontal lines

materials

A fat quarter is an 18″ × 20″–22″ cut of fabric.

HEAVYWEIGHT DOUBLE-SIDED FUSIBLE INTERFACING

18″ bowl: ½ yard or 1 package of fast2fuse HEAVY 20″ × 20″

15″ bowl: ½ yard or 1 package of fast2fuse HEAVY 15″ × 18″

12″ bowl: ⅜ yard or 1 package of fast2fuse HEAVY 15″ × 18″

9″ bowl: ⅜ yard or 1 package of fast2fuse HEAVY 15″ × 18″

FABRIC

Extra fabric may be needed to match a print or stripe.

18″ bowl: ¾ yard

15″ bowl: ⅝ yard

12″ bowl: ½ yard

9″ bowl: ¼ yard or 1 fat quarter

cutting

HEAVYWEIGHT DOUBLE-SIDED FUSIBLE INTERFACING

18″ bowl: Cut 1 square 18″ × 18″.

15″ bowl: Cut 1 square 15″ × 15″.

12″ bowl: Cut 1 square 12″ × 12″.

9″ bowl: Cut 1 square 9″ × 9″.

FABRIC

For a geometric design, the 4 rectangles must be identical.

18″ bowl: Cut 4 rectangles 11″ × 18″.

15″ bowl: Cut 4 rectangles 9½″ × 15″.

12″ bowl: Cut 4 rectangles 8″ × 12″.

9″ bowl: Cut 4 rectangles 6½″ × 9″.

PREPARE THE PATTERN

1. Go to Pattern 1: Mark and Cut Out the Corner Wedges for Corner Seams (page 30).

2. Draw 2 diagonal lines in the center square.

3. With a rotary cutter and quilter's ruler, cut out the 4 corner wedges. Because the interfacing does not ease to fit, number the pieces before you separate them so you know which pieces fit together exactly.

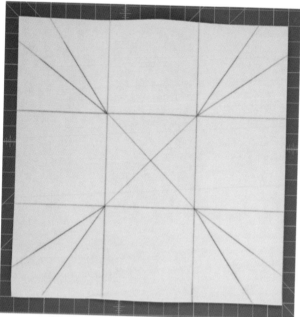

Pattern for triangles

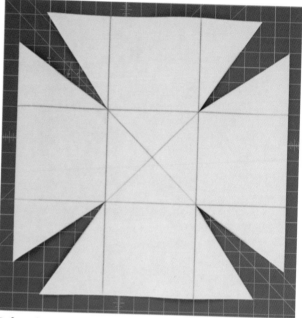

Before diagonal lines are cut

4. Cut the 2 diagonal lines in the center square.

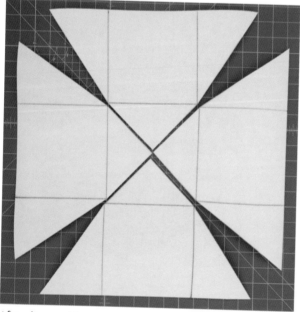

After diagonal lines are cut

FUSE AND TRIM THE FABRIC

Referring to Fusing Fabric to Interfacing (page 13), fuse the fabric to the interfacing and then trim.

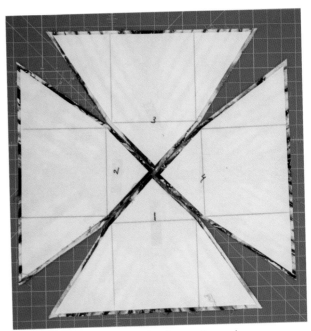

Triangle pieces after fabric has been trimmed

SEW THE SEAMS

1. Line up triangle 1 with triangle 2, fabric sides together, and pin from point A (the tip of the triangle) to point B (the corner of the center square). Make sure the tips of the triangles are lined up. Sew from point A to point B.

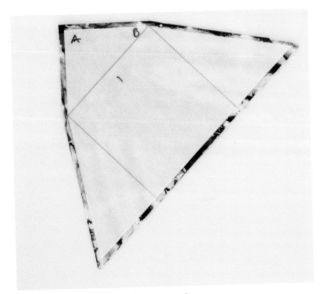

Pin and sew from point A to point B.

2. Repeat to join triangles 3 and 4.

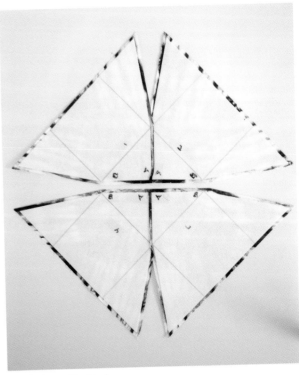

Two halves of inside layer

3. Line up the 2 halves, fabric sides together, so the center seams are aligned at point A. Pin and sew the center square seam from one point B to the opposite point B.

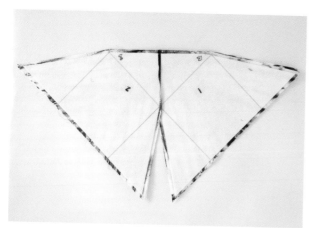

Pinned center seam

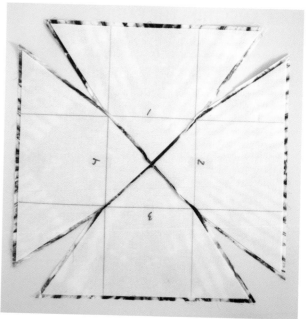

Sewn center seam

4. For quilting the inside layer, refer to Quilting (page 69).

5. Sew the corner seams. See Sew the Seams for a Layer Made with Pattern 1 (page 15).

Inside layer of Fun with Triangles

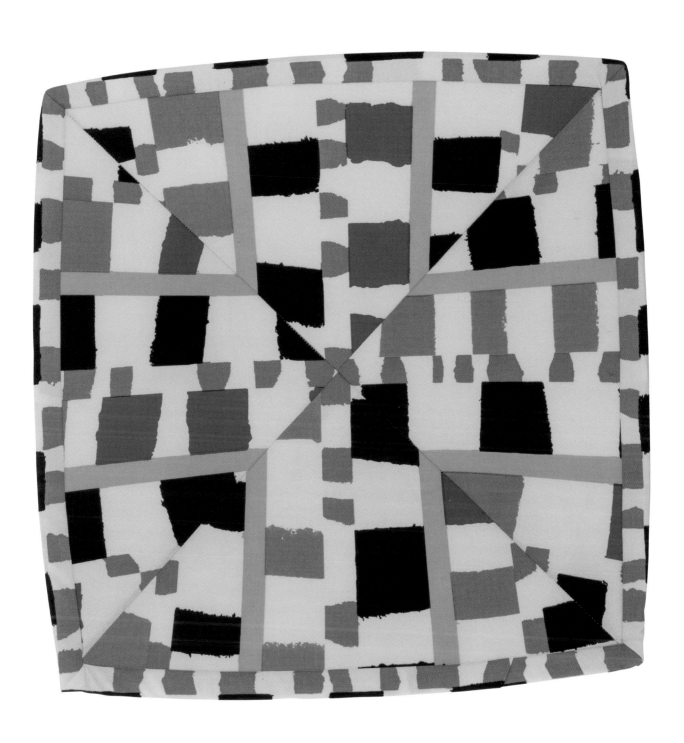

chapter 8

NINE-PATCH BLOCK BOWL 3

In this pattern, there are no corner seams. The three-dimensional shape
is created by the corner diamond shapes.

Novelty fabrics work

well in the pattern.

It is also a great

way to use up scraps.

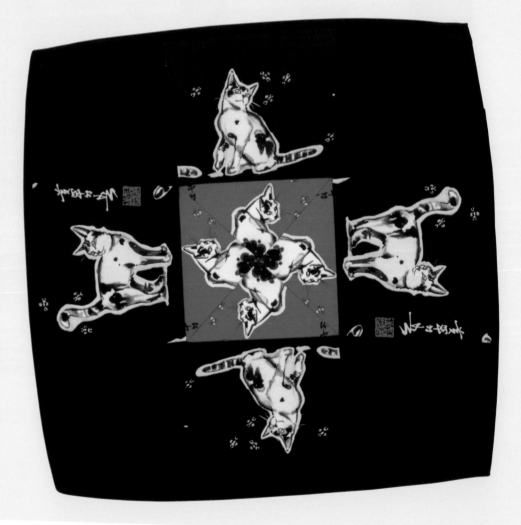

Nine-Patch bowl

materials

A fat quarter is an 18″ × 20″–22″ cut of fabric.

HEAVYWEIGHT DOUBLE-SIDED FUSIBLE INTERFACING

18″ bowl: ½ yard or 1 package of fast2fuse HEAVY 20″ × 20″

15″ bowl: ½ yard or 1 package of fast2fuse HEAVY 15″ × 18″

12″ bowl: ⅜ yard or 1 package of fast2fuse HEAVY 15″ × 18″

9″ bowl: ⅜ yard or 1 package of fast2fuse HEAVY 15″ × 18″

FABRIC

Extra fabric may be needed to match a print or stripe.

18″ bowl: ½ yard

15″ bowl: ⅓ yard

12″ bowl: ⅓ yard or 1 fat quarter

9″ bowl: ¼ yard or 1 fat quarter

cutting

HEAVYWEIGHT DOUBLE-SIDED FUSIBLE INTERFACING

18″ bowl: Cut 1 square 18″ × 18″.

15″ bowl: Cut 1 square 15″ × 15″.

12″ bowl: Cut 1 square 12″ × 12″.

9″ bowl: Cut 1 square 9″ × 9″.

FABRIC

18″ bowl: Cut 9 squares 7″ × 7″.

15″ bowl: Cut 9 squares 6″ × 6″.

12″ bowl: Cut 9 squares 5″ × 5″.

9″ bowl: Cut 9 squares 4″ × 4″.

PREPARE THE PATTERN

Draw and cut out pattern 2 following instructions in Pattern 2: Cut Out the Squares for Diamond Corners (page 31).

All pieces cut out

FUSE AND TRIM THE FABRIC

See Fusing Fabric to Interfacing (page 13). Trim the excess fabric.

If you are working with striped or novelty fabric, refer to Novelty and Striped Fabric (page 59).

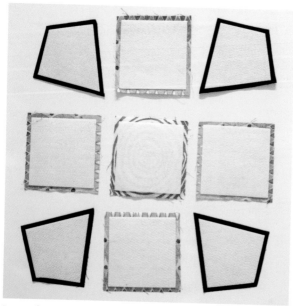

Pieces fused to fabric

SEW THE SEAMS

1. Sew 3 rows of 3 pieces each.

3 rows sewn

NOTE

For quilting the inside layer separately, see Quilting (page 69). Do any quilting before you sew the corner seams but after the center square has been secured.

2. To finish the inside layer, refer to Secure the Center Square and Sew the Seams of the Diamond Shapes (page 17).

Center square secured before final seams are sewn

Inside layer of Nine-Patch bowl

chapter 9
STAR BLOCK BOWL 4

Star blocks work great as the inside design for a bowl; they really let the bowl shine! In this chapter, the directions are for a simple Star block. The pattern can easily be altered to many other Star blocks like the Ohio Star or the Friendship Star. The 18″ bowl looks great with a Star block as the center.

This pattern has no corner seams. The three-dimensional shape is created by the corner diamond shapes. Novelty fabrics work well in the pattern. It is also a great way to use up scraps.

Star Block bowl

materials

A fat quarter is an 18″ × 20″ –22″ cut of fabric.

HEAVYWEIGHT DOUBLE-SIDED FUSIBLE INTERFACING

18″ bowl: ½ yard or 1 package of fast2fuse HEAVY 20″ × 20″

15″ bowl: ½ yard or 1 package of fast2fuse HEAVY 15″ × 18″

12″ bowl: ⅓ yard or 1 package of fast2fuse HEAVY 15″ × 18″

9″ bowl: ¼ yard or 1 package of fast2fuse HEAVY 15″ × 18″

FABRIC

Extra fabric may be needed to match a print or stripe.

18″ bowl: ½ yard

15″ bowl: ⅜ yard

12″ bowl: ⅓ yard or 1 fat quarter

9″ bowl: ⅛ yard or 1 fat quarter

FABRIC FOR STAR POINTS

18″ bowl: ¼ yard or 1 fat quarter

15″ bowl: ¼ yard or 1 fat quarter

12″ bowl: ⅛ yard or 1 fat quarter

9″ bowl: ⅛ yard or 1 fat quarter

cutting

HEAVYWEIGHT DOUBLE-SIDED FUSIBLE INTERFACING

18″ bowl: Cut 1 square 18″ × 18″.

15″ bowl: Cut 1 square 15″ × 15″.

12″ bowl: Cut 1 square 12″ × 12″.

9″ bowl: Cut 1 square 9″ × 9″.

FABRIC

18″ bowl: Cut 9 squares 7″ × 7″.

15″ bowl: Cut 9 squares 6″ × 6″.

12″ bowl: Cut 9 squares 5″ × 5″.

9″ bowl: Cut 9 squares 4″ × 4″.

FABRIC FOR STAR POINTS

If you are working with striped or novelty fabric, see Novelty and Striped Fabric (page 59).

18″ bowl: Cut 8 rectangles 4″ × 7″.

15″ bowl: Cut 8 rectangles 3½″ × 6″.

12″ bowl: Cut 8 rectangles 3″ × 5″.

9″ bowl: Cut 8 rectangles 2½″ × 4″.

PREPARE THE PATTERN

1. Draw and cut out pattern 2 following the instructions in Pattern 2: Cut Out the Squares for Diamond Corners (page 31).

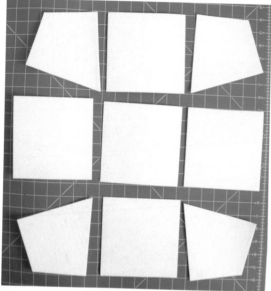

All pieces cut out

2. To draw the star points, mark the midpoint on 4 of the squares and draw a line from that point out to both of the opposite corners.

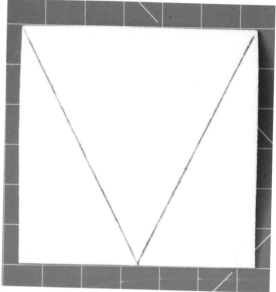

Drawn start points

3. With a quilter's ruler and rotary cutter, cut on the lines.

Altered pattern

FUSE AND TRIM THE FABRIC

See Fusing Fabric to Interfacing (page 13). Trim the excess fabric.

If you are working with striped or novelty fabric, refer to Novelty and Striped Fabric (page 59).

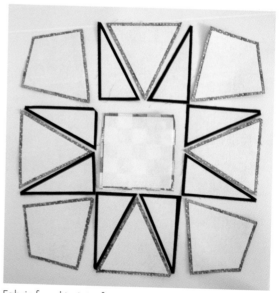

Fabric fused to interfacing

SEW THE SEAMS

1. First make the 4 squares with the triangles.

Square with points

2. Make the top and bottom rows.

Top/bottom row: Make 2.

3. Make the middle row.

Middle row

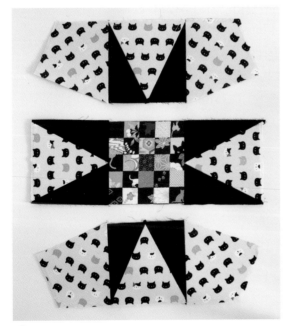

All 3 rows

4. To finish the inside layer, refer to Secure the Center Square and Sew the Seams of the Diamond Shapes (page 17).

> **NOTE**
> For quilting the inside layer separately, go to Quilting (page 69). Do the quilting before you sew the corner seams but after the center square has been secured.

Inside layer of Star Bowl

chapter 10
COMPLETING THE BOWL

After the outside and inside layers are complete, the 2 layers are fused together to create the bowl. The edge of the bowl is finished either with an add-on binding or fold-over binding.

ADD-ON BINDING METHOD

Prepare the Inside and Outside Layers

1. Place the inside layer of the bowl into the outside layer. Press down on the 4 corners at the base of the inside layer.

2. Line up the 4 corners. Also line up the guidelines from the inside layer with the guidelines from the outside layer.

3. The inside layer will be between ⅛″ to ¼″ smaller than the outside layer, depending on the size of the bowl and also the design of the inside layer.

4. Pin at the corners and along the edges of all 4 sides of the bowl.

Outside and inside layers pinned together

Fuse the Layers Together

The 2 layers are fused together from the inside of the bowl.

1. Start to fuse from the center of one of the 4 sides and fuse out towards the corner. Remove the pins as you go.

TIP *If your iron has automatic turn off, keep it slowly moving during fusing so it does not turn off.*

2. Fuse for 15–20 seconds, depending on the iron, before moving the iron to the next spot. *Do not press down on the iron.* That will leave indentation marks.

3. The fabric will be damp after being fused. Press each side dry before moving to the next side.

TIP *To determine the time it takes to fuse the inside layer and outside layer together, fuse fabric to 2 of the leftover corner wedges of interfacing. Then time how long it takes to fuse the 2 wedges together.*

> **NOTE**
> It is not necessary to fuse the base of the bowl. However, you can do so if you have a small travel iron.

TIP *fast2fuse HEAVY Interfacing uses an iron-on cotton setting with steam. To avoid burn marks on your fabric, use a dry pressing cloth to protect the bowl.*

> **NOTE**
> An iron with a higher voltage will fuse faster that an iron with a lower voltage. Keep that in mind when determining the time it will take to fuse the 2 layers together.

Trim the Edge

With a rotary cutter, trim the edge of the outside layer even with the edge of the inside layer's fabric.

Bind the Bowl

materials

BINDING FABRIC

Extra fabric may be needed to match a print or stripe.

18″ bowl: ¼ yard for straight-grain binding *or* ½ yard for bias binding

15″ bowl: ¼ yard for straight-grain binding *or* ½ yard for bias binding

12″ bowl: ¼ yard for straight-grain binding *or* ½ yard for bias binding

9″ bowl: ⅛ yard for straight-grain binding *or* ½ yard for bias binding

EXTRAS

30-weight thread

Machine sewing needle size 90/14 or 100/16

Pressing cloth

cutting

BINDING FABRIC

18″ bowl: Cut 2 strips 2½″ × width of fabric for straight binding, *or* cut 3 strips 2½″ wide on the bias to make a 65″ binding strip.

15″ bowl: Cut 2 strips 2½″ × width of fabric for straight binding, *or* cut 3 strips 2½″ wide on the bias to make a 56″ binding strip.

12″ bowl: Cut 2 strips 2½″ × width of fabric for straight binding, *or* cut 2 strips 2½″ wide on the bias to make a 46″ binding strip.

9″ bowl: Cut 1 strip 2½″ × width of fabric for straight binding, *or* cut 2 strips 2½″ wide on the bias to make a 37″ binding strip.

Prepare the Binding

1. Cut one end of the binding at a 45° angle. Fold ¼″ of the end under, wrong sides together, and press.

2. Fold the binding in half, with the right side of the fabric out. Press.

Sew on the Binding

1. Start with the tip of the binding in the middle of one side. Pin the binding to the inside of the bowl with the raw edge of the binding running along the edge of the bowl.

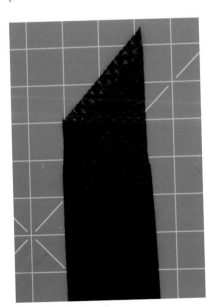

Folded end of binding

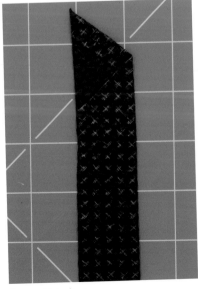

Pressed binding

Beginning point for binding

2. Sew the binding on using a ¼″ seam allowance. Begin to sew 3½″ from the tip of the binding.

3. Stop ¼″ from the tip of the corner. End with the needle down.

TIP *To get a precise corner, use a pencil to mark the 1/4″ spot to stop.*

4. Rotate the bowl and sew a diagonal line in a 45° angle to the tip of the corner.

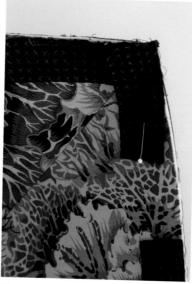

Corner seam

5. Fold the binding so the raw edge runs along the side to be sewn next.

Folded binding corner

6. Start to sew from the edge.

Beginning of next seam

7. Continue until all 4 corners are done.

8. Sew to 1″ from the beginning of the binding and cut off the remaining binding, leaving a 3″ tail.

9. Tuck the end of the binding into the beginning of the binding and pin.

End tucked into beginning

10. Finish sewing the binding to the bowl.

Finish the Binding

Turn the folded edge of the binding to the outside of the bowl. Pin it and stitch it down, either by hand or machine.

Corner of add-on binding

Finished binding

FOLD-OVER BINDING METHOD

Prepare the Inside Layer

1. Fold the extra ¼″ of fabric to the interfacing side. Pin it from the fabric side.

Folded fabric edge of inside layer

2. Place the inside layer on a nonstick surface on your ironing board, interfacing side down, and fuse the ¼″ fabric edge to the interfacing. Remove the pins as you go.

Fuse edge of fabric to interfacing side.

Prepare the Outside Layer

1. Fold the fabric to the interfacing side. With the tip of an iron, fuse the fabric to the interfacing.

Outside layer's fabric fused to interfacing side

2. At the corners, fold down the next side, pin, and continue fusing. Because the corners are not 90°, the folds will not be lined up with the corner seams.

Folded corner

Fuse the Layers Together

The 2 layers are fused together from the inside of the bowl. Place the inside layer into the outside layer, with the corner seams lined up, and pin the 2 layers together.

Inside and outside layers pinned together

Follow the instructions in Add–On Binding Method, Fuse the Layers Together (page 52).

Stitch the Edge

Stitch the edge of the inside layer to the outside layer either by hand or machine. If it is done by machine, the stitching will be visible on both the inside and the outside of the bowl.

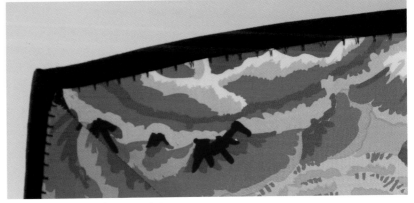

Inside layer stitched to outside layer

chapter 11
VARIATIONS

This chapter has techniques on how to individualize a bowl. This can be done by using novelty or striped fabric; by adding appliqué, embroidery, or "hang-overs" to the inside layer; or by quilting the bowl. You also have the option of adding a protective finish to your bowl.

NOVELTY AND STRIPED FABRIC

Novelty fabric

When using novelty or striped fabric, the placement of the interfacing on the fabric is critical. Because you cannot see the interfacing when fusing it to the fabric, it is important that the interfacing is placed correctly on the wrong side of the fabric before the two are fused together.

Working with Novelty Fabric

1. To determine the exact image to use, cut out a window from a piece of paper in the shape of the interfacing piece, and move the paper around on the fabric until you find the perfect image. If you want to repeat the same image several times, make marks on the paper frame where the image meets the frame.

Selected image

2. With a pencil, outline the shape of the interfacing on the wrong side of the fabric.

TIP *If you cannot see the image on the wrong side of the fabric, sew a running stitch around the image on the right side of the fabric.*

Outlined image

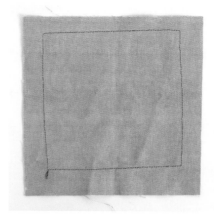

Image outlined with a running stitch

3. Use the pencil or sewing lines as your guide for positioning the interfacing on the wrong side of the fabric. Use blue painter's tape to fasten the interfacing piece onto the wrong side of fabric so it is within the pencil or sewing lines.

Interfacing taped to fabric

4. Press the interfacing to the fabric; then remove the tape.

5. Securely fuse the fabric and interfacing together.

Working with Stripes

Striped fabric can create a very dramatic bowl. These directions show how they are used for pattern 2.

Working with Vertical Lines

1. To get the stripes to meet in the center of the bowl, mark a center-line on each of the 4 interfacing triangles.

2. Line up the centerline of the interfacing with the fabric stripe you want in the center of the bowl.

3. Use blue painter's tape to fasten the interfacing to the wrong side of the fabric. Press, remove the tape, and then securely fuse.

Interfacing with vertical lines, taped to wrong side of striped fabric

Working with Horizontal Lines

1. Draw horizontal guidelines on each of the 4 interfacing pieces.

2. Line up the guidelines with the lines on the fabric, and tape the interfacing to the wrong side of the fabric. Press, remove the tape, and then securely fuse.

Interfacing with horizontal lines taped to fabric

APPLIQUÉ AND EMBROIDERY

Appliqué and embroidery work great as design elements for the inside of a fabric bowl. Just keep in mind the bowl is three-dimensional with no up, down, left, or right when you plan the design.

African Animals 1, by Dorah Hlongwane and Stella Mnisi

TIP *Before you add appliqué fabric or embroidery thread to the fabric, check to make sure it is color fast, so the colors do not "run" when the fabric is fused to the interfacing.*

Appliqué and embroidery are added to the fabric before it is fused to the interfacing. To ensure the design does not get lost in the corner seams, mark the outline of the interfacing on the fabric.

General Appliqué and Embroidery Instructions

materials

A fat quarter is an 18" × 20"–22" cut of fabric.

HEAVYWEIGHT DOUBLE-SIDED FUSIBLE INTERFACING

18" bowl: ½ yard or 1 package of fast2fuse HEAVY 20" × 20"

15" bowl: ½ yard or 1 package of fast2fuse HEAVY 15" × 18"

12" bowl: ⅓ yard or 1 package of fast2fuse HEAVY 15" × 18"

9" bowl: ¼ yard or 1 package of fast2fuse HEAVY 15" × 18"

BACKGROUND FABRIC

Extra fabric may be needed to match a print or stripe.

18" bowl: ⅝ yard

15" bowl: ½ yard or 1 fat quarter

12" bowl: ⅜ yard or 1 fat quarter

9" bowl: ⅓ yard or 1 fat quarter

EXTRAS FOR APPLIQUÉ

Fabric for appliqué: Scraps

Fusible web

Threads to sew appliqué to background fabric

EXTRAS FOR EMBROIDERY

Embroidery thread

cutting

HEAVYWEIGHT DOUBLE-SIDED FUSIBLE INTERFACING

18″ bowl: Cut 1 square 18″ × 18″.

15″ bowl: Cut 1 square 15″ × 15″.

12″ bowl: Cut 1 square 12″ × 12″.

9″ bowl: Cut 1 square 9″ × 9″.

BACKGROUND FABRIC

18″ bowl: Cut 1 square 19″ × 19″.

15″ bowl: Cut 1 square 16″ × 16″.

12″ bowl: Cut 1 square 13″ × 13″.

9″ bowl: Cut 1 square 10″ × 10″.

Cut Out the Interfacing

Go to Pattern 1: Mark and Cut Out the Corner Wedges for Corner Seams (page 30).

Mark and Embellish the Fabric

1. Tape the interfacing to the wrong side of the fabric.

2. With a fabric marker, draw a line all the way around the edge of the interfacing, including the inside the corners.

3. With contrasting thread, sew a running stitch on the outline of the interfacing. Also sew a running stitch to outline the center square. This will be very useful when you lay out your design.

4. Add appliqué or embroidery in the area inside the outline.

Outlined area with embroidery: African Animals 2, by Kelelo Maepa and Christina Mabasa

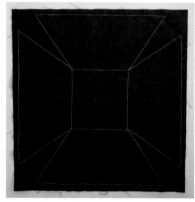

Outlined appliqué or embroidery area

Fuse and Finish

1. Tape the interfacing to the wrong side of the appliquéd or embroidered fabric with the guidelines up. Make sure the interfacing is within the area outlined by the running stitches.

Interfacing taped to wrong side of embellished fabric

2. Fuse the fabric and the interfacing together. See Fusing Fabric to Interfacing (page 13).

3. Remove the running stitches.

4. With a rotary cutter and quilter's ruler, trim the fabric to ¼″ from outer edge of the interfacing. *Do not trim inside the corner wedges.*

5. To complete the inside layer of the bowl, refer to Sew the Seams for a Layer Made with Pattern 1 (page 15).

Sample Pattern for Raw-Edge Appliqué

Appliquéd inside bowl

materials

A fat quarter is an 18″ × 20″–22″ cut of fabric.

HEAVYWEIGHT DOUBLE-SIDED FUSIBLE INTERFACING

18″ bowl: ½ yard or 1 package of fast2fuse HEAVY 20″ × 20″

15″ bowl: ½ yard or 1 package of fast2fuse HEAVY 15″ × 18″

12″ bowl: ⅓ yard or 1 package of fast2fuse HEAVY 15″ × 18″

9″ bowl: ¼ yard or 1 package of fast2fuse HEAVY 15″ × 18″

BACKGROUND FABRIC

18″ bowl: ⅝ yard

15″ bowl: ½ yard or 1 fat quarter

12″ bowl: ⅜ yard or 1 fat quarter

9″ bowl: ⅓ yard or 1 fat quarter

CONTRASTING FABRIC FOR APPLIQUÉ

18″ bowl: ⅝ yard

15″ bowl: ½ yard or 1 fat quarter

12″ bowl: ⅜ yard or 1 fat quarter

9″ bowl: ⅓ yard or 1 fat quarter

LIGHTWEIGHT FUSIBLE WEB

18″ bowl: ½ yard

15″ bowl: ½ yard

12″ bowl: ⅓ yard

9″ bowl: ¼ yard

> **NOTE**
> For the 18″ bowl, I use 21″–wide fusible web from FlexiFuse.

EXTRAS

Thread for sewing appliqué onto background fabric

Small sharp scissors to cut out appliqué pattern

Removable fabric marker

Copy machine or pencil

cutting

HEAVYWEIGHT DOUBLE-SIDED FUSIBLE INTERFACING

18″ bowl: Cut 1 square 18″ × 18″.

15″ bowl: Cut 1 square 15″ × 15″.

12″ bowl: Cut 1 square 12″ × 12″.

9″ bowl: Cut 1 square 9″ × 9″.

BACKGROUND FABRIC

18″ bowl: Cut 1 square 19″ × 19″.

15″ bowl: Cut 1 square 16″ × 16″.

12″ bowl: Cut 1 square 13″ × 13″.

9″ bowl: Cut 1 square 10″ × 10″.

CONTRASTING FABRIC FOR APPLIQUÉ

18″ bowl: Cut 1 square 19″ × 19″.

15″ bowl: Cut 1 square 16″ × 16″.

12″ bowl: Cut 1 square 13″ × 13″.

9″ bowl: Cut 1 square 10″ × 10″.

LIGHTWEIGHT FUSIBLE WEB

18″ bowl: Cut 1 square 18″ × 18″.

15″ bowl: Cut 1 square 15″ × 15″.

12″ bowl: Cut 1 square 12″ × 12″.

9″ bowl: Cut 1 square 9″ × 9″.

Cut Out the Interfacing

Go to Pattern 1: Mark and Cut Out the Corner Wedges for Corner Seams (page 30).

Mark the Background Fabric and Fusible Web

1. Tape the interfacing to the wrong side of the background fabric.

2. With a fabric marker, draw a line all the way around the edge of the interfacing, including the inside the corners.

3. Draw the horizontal and vertical centerlines.

18″ bowl: Draw the centerlines 9″ from the edges.

15″ bowl: Draw the centerlines 7½″ from the edges.

12″ bowl: Draw the centerlines 6″ from the edges.

9″ bowl: Draw the centerlines 4½″ from the edges.

4. With contrasting thread, sew a running stitch on the outline of the interfacing and the horizontal and vertical centerlines on the fabric.

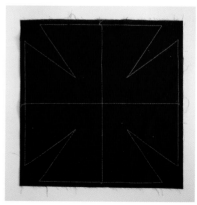

Outlined appliqué area and centerlines

Transfer the Pattern to Fusible Web

1. Go to Template and Appliqué Patterns (page 74) to find the pattern for the bowl size you are making. Copy the pattern onto paper. Use the darkest ink setting on a copy machine, or trace with a pencil.

2. On the paper side of the fusible web, draw a square the same size as the bowl you are making. So for an 18″ bowl, draw an 18″ square.

3. Mark the center horizontal and vertical lines. *For the 18″ bowl only,* draw 2 additional diagonal lines.

4. Cover the pattern with the fusible web so the dashed centerlines of the pattern are lined up with the centerlines on the fusible web. *For the 18″ bowl only,* line up the dashed line with the diagonal line.

5. With a pencil, trace the pattern onto the first quarter of the fusible web.

6. Line up the pattern with the next quarter of the fusible web and trace it again.

Trace the pattern.

Tracing on second quarter

Pattern lined up with centerlines on fusible web

TIP *Use blue painter's tape to hold the pattern in place.*

7. Trace the pattern onto the 2 remaining quarters of the fusible web.

Entire pattern traced to fusible web

NOTE

For the 18″ bowl only, the pattern will be 4 quarters with diagonal lines.

Transfer the Fusible Web to Appliqué Fabric

1. Fuse the fusible web to the wrong side of the appliqué fabric, following the manufacturer's directions.

2. Cut out the pattern on the marked lines.

3. With a heat-removable fabric marker, draw horizontal and vertical centerlines on the right side of the appliqué fabric (not necessary for the 18″ bowl).

Cutout appliqué with centerlines marked

Appliqué the Fabric

1. Remove the fusible web paper from the wrong side of the appliqué.

2. Line up the horizontal and vertical stitched centerlines on the background fabric with the horizontal and vertical lines on the appliqué fabric.

Appliqué lined up on background fabric

Centerlines aligned

3. Make sure the appliqué fabric is within the outline on the background fabric.

4. Fuse the appliqué to the right side of the background fabric.

5. Remove the horizontal and vertical stitched lines.

6. With a decorative stitch, either by hand or machine, sew down the appliqué edges.

Complete the Layer

1. Fuse the fabric and the interfacing together. See Fusing Fabric to Interfacing (page 13).

2. With a rotary cutter and quilter's ruler, trim the fabric to ¼″ from the outer edge of the interfacing. *Do not trim inside the corner wedges.*

3. To finish the inside layer of the bowl, refer to Sew the Seams for a Layer Made with Pattern 1 (page 15).

ADDING "HANG-OVERS"

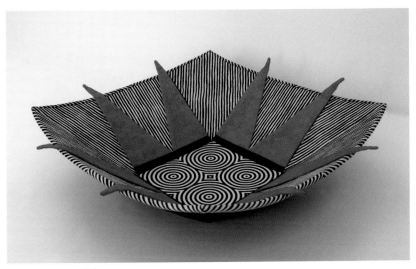

Star pattern with hang-overs

One way to add another dimension to a bowl is to insert decorative hang-overs. The hang-overs are sewn into the seams when the pieces for the inside layer are sewn together. The hang-overs can be any shape you want, such as leaves or triangles. I have provided patterns for triangle hang-overs, but you can also design your own.

NOTE
Add any decorative stitches to the hang-overs before they are sewn into the seam.

materials for the hangovers

A fat quarter is an 18" × 20"–22" cut of fabric.

FABRIC

18" bowl: ⅓ yard or 1 fat quarter

15" bowl: ¼ yard or 1 fat quarter

12" bowl: ¼ yard or 1 fat quarter

9" bowl: ¼ yard or 1 fat quarter

TEMPLATE PLASTIC

1 sheet 8½" × 11"

cutting

Make a triangle template by tracing the triangle pattern (pages 75–78) for the bowl size you are making onto template plastic.

FABRIC

Cut 8 triangles and 8 reverse triangles with the template.

1 set of triangles

TIP *If you fold the fabric right sides together and mark and cut 8 pieces in the shape of the template, you will have 8 sets each of 2 opposite pieces.*

Make the Triangles

1. Sew 2 triangles right sides together along the 2 long sides. Use a ¼" seam allowance. Do not sew the side of the triangle that gets sewn into the seam. Make 8 triangles.

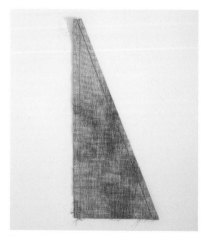

Triangle sewn together

2. Turn the triangles right side out.

Attach the Triangles

1. Line up the unsewn edge of 2 triangles with the edge of the bowl piece. The sides of the triangles should be ¼" from the edge of the bowl piece so they don't get caught in seams. The triangles overlap in the center of the piece.

Hang-overs lined up with the bowl piece

2. Lay the adjacent bowl piece on top of the triangles. This will sandwich the triangles between the 2 bowl pieces. Pin close to the interfacing.

3. Sew the pieces together right along the edge of the interfacing.

4. Continue to sew the bowl pieces together, adding hangovers at the appropriate seams.

Sew right along the interfacing.

Finished seam

QUILTING

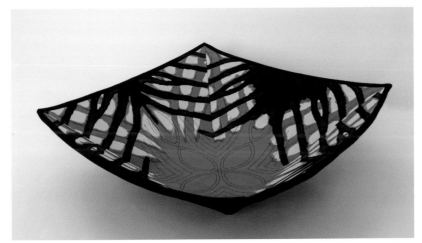

Quilting design by Roberta Benvin for Quilting Creations International

Quilted inside bowl

Fabric bowls do not have to be quilted because the inside layer and outside layer are fused together to create the bowl. However, you may want to add quilting for additional detail.

The inside and outside layers can be quilted separately before they are fused together. This can be done from either the interfacing side or the fabric side.

The bowl can also be quilted after the 2 layers have been fused together. A bowl where the 2 layers are already fused will not bend. Depending on the sewing machine and the size of the bowl, you might not be able to quilt the center of a pre-fused bowl.

materials

Sewing needles size 80/14 or 90/100

30- or 40-weight thread: Check to make sure the thread is strong enough to sew through a layer of heavyweight interfacing.

30- or 40-weight bobbin thread *or* **decorative thread** that can be used in the bobbin and can sew through a layer of heavyweight interfacing

Marking tools: Pencil for marking interfacing side and heat-removable marker for marking fabric side

> **NOTE**
> Make sure your threads are colorfast and will not bleed when the inside and outside layers are fused together.

> **NOTE**
> Do not use a water-soluble fabric marker. It will undo the glue on the interfacing when it is removed.

TIP Fuse a piece of scrap fabric to the leftover interfacing wedges. Use that piece to regulate the tension on the sewing machine and to check which needle to use.

Quilting the Outside and Inside Layers Separately

The inside layer and outside layer can be quilted from either the fabric side or the interfacing side.

Quilting from the Interfacing Side

MARK THE QUILTING LINES

Use a pencil to draw the lines for the quilting pattern before the corner seams are sewn. Only the lines on the interfacing will be seen. It is the bobbin thread that will be seen on the fabric side.

Marked quilting lines

After the first stitch, pull up the bobbin thread so it does not get caught in the stitching.

Quilting from the Fabric Side

MARK THE QUILTING LINES

Use a heat-removable fabric marker to draw the quilting pattern. Keep in mind that the fabric in the corners without interfacing will not be visible after the corner seams have been sewn.

Quilt the layer; then remove all marked lines before the inside layer and outside layer are fused together. Note that the center square of the outside layer will not be visible when the bowl is finished.

Suggested Pattern for the Outside Layer

After the interfacing for the outside layer has been cut out and fused to the fabric but before the corner seams have been sewn together, draw horizontal and vertical centerlines on the interfacing.

18″ bowl: Draw the lines 9½″ from the edge of the interfacing.

15″ bowl: Draw the lines 8″ from the edge of the interfacing.

12″ bowl: Draw the lines 6½″ from the edge of the interfacing.

9″ bowl: Draw the lines 5″ from the edge of the interfacing.

Next, draw quilting lines ½″ apart from the corner interfacing edges to the centerline of each of the 4 sides. Make sure the lines meet at the centerline. Do not draw quilting lines inside the center square.

Quilting pattern for outside layer

Quilted outside layer

NOTE
The center square of the outside layer will not be seen, so design the quilting pattern accordingly.

Quilting a Pre-Fused Bowl

A bowl in which the outside and inside layers are already fused can only be quilted from the inside. Measure the space on your machine from the needle to the right to make sure there is enough space to quilt the bowl center.

Mark the quilting lines with a heat-removable fabric marker. Start and end your stitching at the edge of the bowl so you can secure the ends of your thread in the binding, where the fabric is not fused to the interfacing. Be patient—it can be difficult to free-motion quilt through 2 layers of fused heavyweight interfacing.

TIP *Fuse 2 pieces of leftover interfacing to fabric. Then fuse them together. Use that piece to regulate the tension on the sewing machine and to decide on which size needle to use.*

ADDING A PROTECTIVE FINISH

Lacquered bowl

These bowls are primarily meant to be used for decoration. However, if you want to add a protective layer, that can be done after the inside and outside layers have been fused together. A protective layer can also be used to secure a design that is very difficult to sew.

materials

Decoupage medium (I like Mod Podge.)

Sponge brush

Regular painter's brush

Water-based protective coating (I like Polycrylic Protective Finish by Minwax.)

Fine sandpaper

Fabric test of Mod Podge and water-based protectant

TIP *Before applying the finish to the bowl, test the decoupage medium and the water-based protectant on some scraps of the fabric to see how it responds. The Mod Podge will slightly change the color of the fabric.*

1. Dilute the decoupage medium with water in a 3-to-1 ratio.

2. Use a sponge brush to apply a thin layer of the decoupage solution to the inside of the bowl. Let it dry. Apply a second layer. If the surface is uneven, you can sand it down with a piece of fine sandpaper.

NOTE
The decoupage solution will prevent the water-based protectant from being absorbed by the interfacing.

3. After the second layer of decoupage solution has dried, apply a thin layer of the water-based protectant with a brush.

TIP *Because the sides of the bowl do not lay horizontal, it is better to apply several thin layers of the protectant instead of thicker layers. Use sandpaper in between each layer if needed.*

TIP *There are many options for using different design elements. It is a good idea to make a small sample before you do the final bowl.*

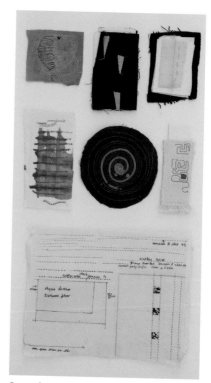

Samples using different design elements

GALLERY

Double Ohio Star, by Kirsten Fisher

Appliquéd Center Square, by Kirsten Fisher

Paul's Bowl, by Paul Felski (acrylic paint and pencil)

Spinning Star, by Martha McDonald

Playing with Patches, by Pat Olsen

Skyscraper, by Christine Janove

template and appliqué
PATTERNS

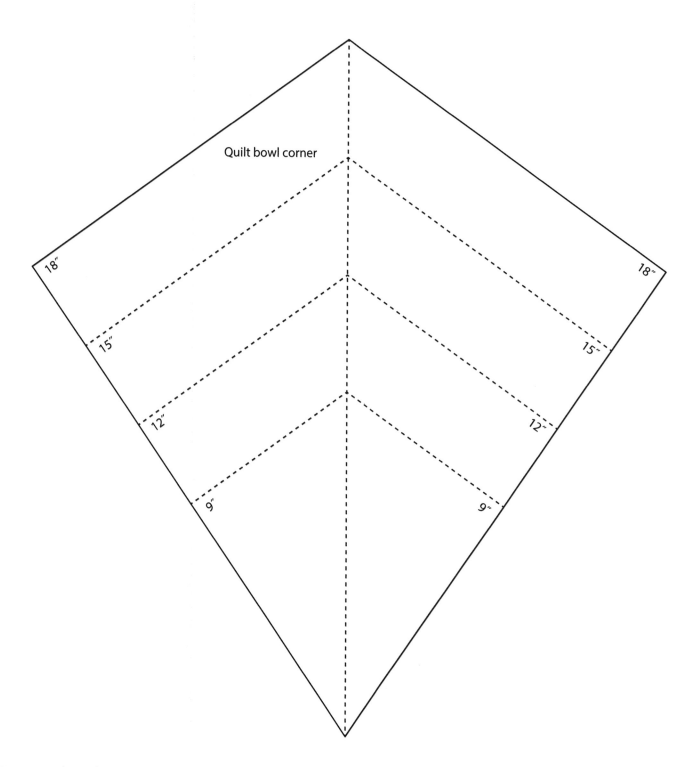

Quilt bowl corner

18" 18"

15" 15"

12" 12"

9" 9"

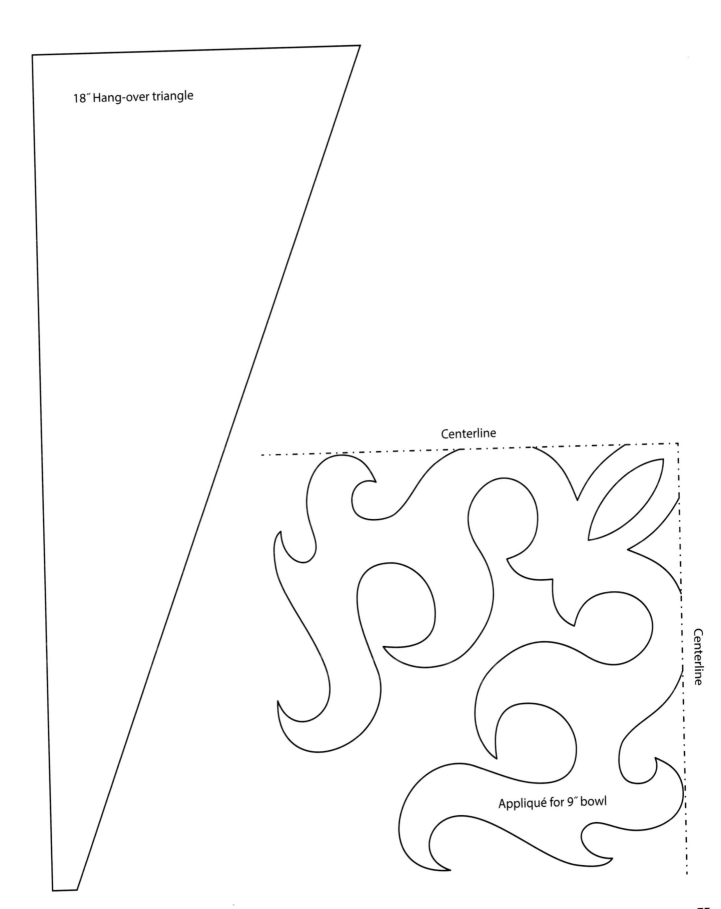

18″ Hang-over triangle

Centerline

Centerline

Appliqué for 9″ bowl

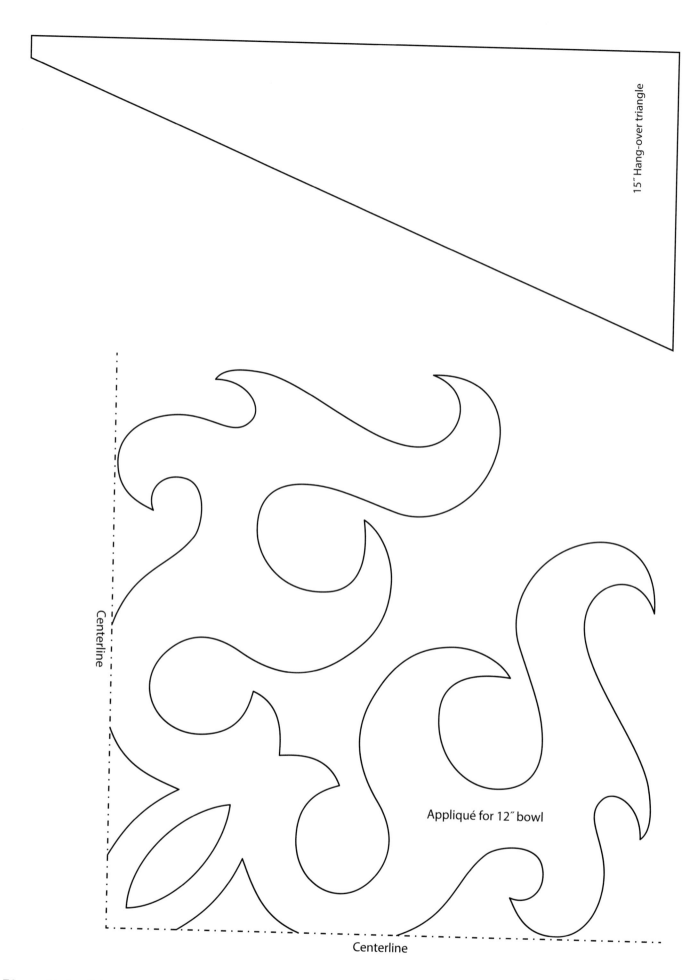

15" Hang-over triangle

Centerline

Appliqué for 12˝ bowl

Centerline

9″ Hang-over triangle

Centerline

Appliqué for 15″ bowl

Centerline

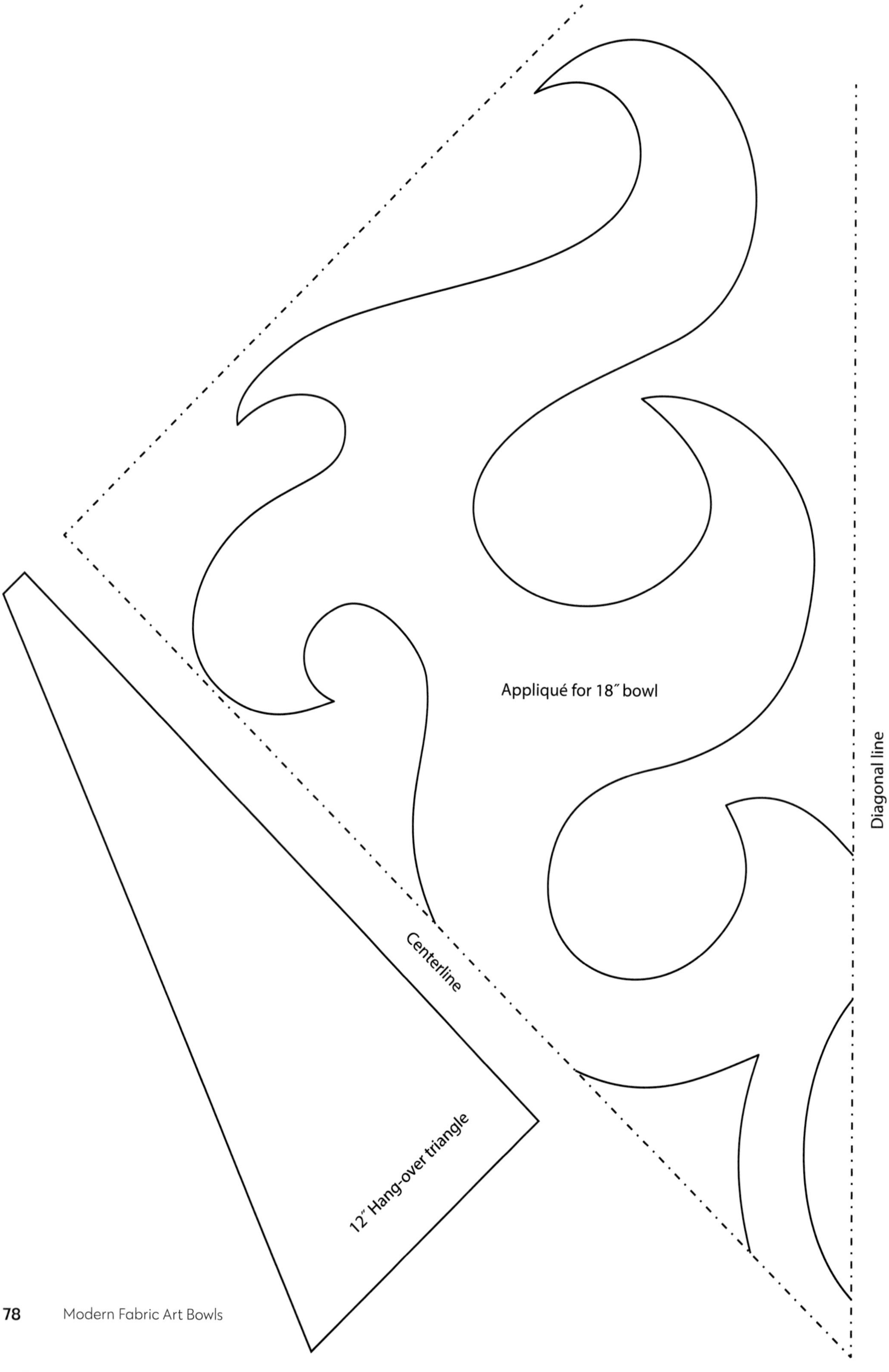

Appliqué for 18″ bowl

Diagonal line

Centerline

12″ Hang-over triangle

about the AUTHOR

Craft has been part of Kirsten's life since she was five years old. Her first project was a pillowcase made out of a *karklud*, a Danish cleaning cloth with very loose loops that you can pull a string of yarn through. Kirsten's grandmother taught her how to knit at the age of seven. Sewing and knitting have been a part of Kirsten's life ever since.

In Denmark, where she grew up, sewing was taught in the schools, and by the age of fourteen, Kirsten sewed a lot of her own clothes. When she moved to Brooklyn, New York, in 1977, her first sewing project was her wedding dress. It was made from curtains her grandmother had painted for her apartment in Copenhagen. After that, her mother-in-law bought her a sewing machine.

In 1983, Kirsten came upon The Brooklyn Quilters Guild show and fell in love with quilting. Creating beautiful, usable objects really appealed to her. At the same time, quilting allowed her to explore the endless possibilities of a 12″ square.

Kirsten has been teaching quilting and bowl making for more than ten years. She is a member and former copresident of The Brooklyn Quilters Guild and is a member of The Textile Study Group of New York.

Visit Kirsten online and follow on social media!

Website: kirstenfisher.net

Instagram: @7willowstudio

Photo by MG Vander Elst

RESOURCES

Quilt Bowl Corner acrylic template
kirstenfisher.net

fast2fuse HEAVY Interfacing
ctpub.com

Marimekko fabric
marimekko.com

FlexiFuse
flexifuse.com